KINGFISHER
READERS

level
1

Ladybugs

Thea Feldman

KINGFISHER

NEW YORK

KINGFISHER
LONDON & NEW YORK

Copyright © Kingfisher 2015
Published in the United States by Kingfisher,
175 Fifth Ave., New York, NY 10010
Kingfisher is an imprint of Pan Macmillan, London.
All rights reserved.

Distributed in the U.S. and Canada by Macmillan,
175 Fifth Ave., New York, NY 10010

Library of Congress Cataloging-in-Publication data
has been applied for.

Series editor: Thea Feldman
Literacy consultant: Ellie Costa, Bank Street College, New York

978-0-7534-7219-4 (HB)
978-0-7534-7220-0 (PB)

Kingfisher books are available for special promotions
and premiums. For details contact: Special Markets
Department, Macmillan, 175 Fifth Ave., New York, NY 10010.

For more information, please visit
www.kingfisherbooks.com

Printed in China

9 8 7 6 5 4 3 2 1
1TR/0315/WKT/UG/115MA

Picture credits
The Publisher would like to thank the following for permission to reproduce their material.
Top = t; Bottom = b; Center = c; Left = l; Right = r
Cover Shutterstock/ninii; Pages 3 Shutterstock/chris2766; 4–5 Shutterstock/PHOTO FUN;
5 Naturepl/Rod Williams; 6 Shutterstock/SJ Allen; 7 Shutterstock/Katarina Christenson;
8–9 Nature/Chris Shields (WAC); 10 Shutterstock/PHOTO FUN; 11 Shutterstock/Henrik Larsson;
12–13 Shutterstock/Zigzag Mountain Art; 14–15 Frank Lane Picture Agency (FLPA)/Albert de
Wilde; 15 Naturepl/Doug Wechsler; 16t Shutterstock/PHOTO FUN; 16–17 Shutterstock/Christian
Musat; 18 Flickr/muffinn; 19t Flickr/Gilles San Martin; 19b Flickr/Jean-Daniel Echenard;
20 Naturepl/Doug Wechsler; 21 Shutterstock/PHOTO FUN; 22–23 Naturepl/Rolf Nussbaumer;
24 Naturepl/Rolf Nussbaumer; 25 Naturepl/Nick Upton; 26 Naturepl/Meul/ARCO;
27 Shutterstock/Dimijana; 28 Shutterstock/Steve Shoup; 29t Shutterstock/Arsgera;
29b Shutterstock/Vasca; 30t Shutterstock/trucic; 30b Shutterstock/Christian Musat;
31t Shutterstock/stoupa; 31b Shutterstock/Maria Uspenskaya.

Look at the **insect** on this leaf.

It is a ladybug!

Many ladybugs are red
with black spots.

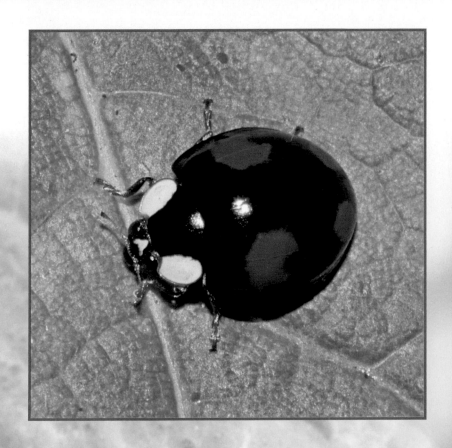

A lot of ladybugs are black
with red spots!

Some ladybugs have no
spots at all.

Some ladybugs have stripes!

There are about
5,000 kinds of ladybug.

Most ladybugs have
bright colors.

The colors warn other animals not to eat ladybugs.

Ladybugs have **poison** in them that can make other animals sick.

What do ladybugs eat?
Ladybugs eat **aphids**
(say "ay-fidz").

Aphids are insects too.

Aphids eat plants in gardens and farms.

Aphids are not good for plants. People call aphids **pests**.

Not all ladybugs
are female!
There are male
ladybugs too.

male

Most female ladybugs
are a little bigger
than male ones.

female

A ladybug lays eggs
on a plant where
aphids live.

Then she leaves.

After four to seven days,
the eggs **hatch**.

A baby ladybug
does not look like
a grown-up ladybug.

A baby ladybug is hungry!

As soon as it hatches,
a baby ladybug starts
to eat aphids.

It can eat 25 aphids a day.

A baby ladybug grows.

It grows so much it becomes too big for its skin!

The skin splits
and falls off.

The ladybug has a new
skin that fits better.

This happens a few times.

When a ladybug is
two or three weeks old,
it holds on to a leaf.

The ladybug's skin splits open
one more time.

Now there is a hard case
that covers the ladybug.

After about five more days,
the case breaks open.

A grown-up ladybug
comes out.

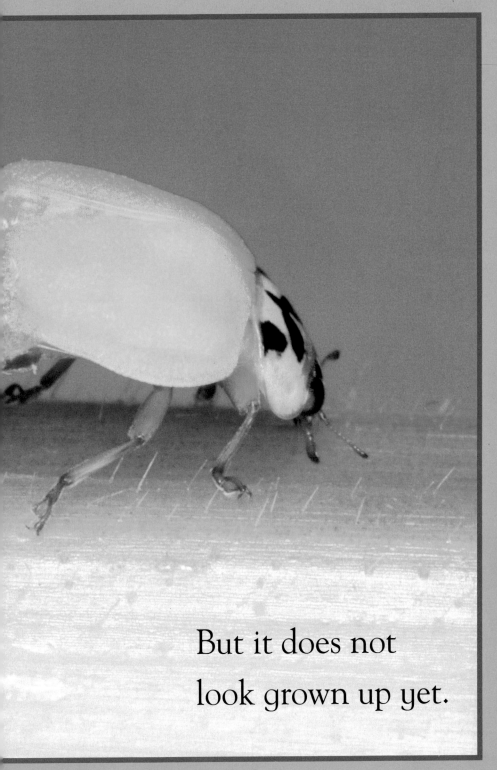

But it does not
look grown up yet.

A grown-up ladybug comes out with a soft shell.

The soft shell will be hard in a few hours.

The color of the shell
will change too.

A ladybug's shell
covers its wings.

A ladybug opens its shell
and lifts its wings to fly!

Where is the ladybug going?

Maybe it is going to eat aphids.

A grown-up ladybug can eat more than 50 aphids a day.

Ladybugs spend **winter** out of sight in large groups to stay warm.

Ladybugs come out again
when the weather
gets warmer.

When we see ladybugs
we know **spring** is on the way.

Ladybugs will help
take care of plant pests.

Ladybugs have bright colors and are pretty.

Some people say ladybugs bring good luck!

What do you think?

Glossary

aphid a tiny insect that eats plants

hatch to break out of an egg and be born

insect a small animal with six legs

pest an animal that bothers other animals, plants, or people

poison something that can make animals sick or even kill them

spring the time of year that comes after winter, when the weather starts to get warmer

winter the coldest time of the year

 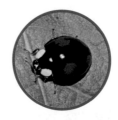